W9-CRX-248

Ðisnep · PIXAR

TOP 10s
IT'S DRIVE TIME!

MARY LINDEEN

For Benjamin, who led me to the joy of cars and Cars

Lerner Publications Company
A division of Lerner Publishing Group, Inc.
241 First Avenue North
Minneapolis, MN 55401 USA

For reading levels and more information, look up this title at
www.lernerbooks.com.

Main body text set in ITC Avant Garde Gothic 13/14.
Typeface provided by International Typeface Corp.

Library of Congress Cataloging-in-Publication Data

The Cataloging-in-Publication Data for *Cars Top 10s: It's Drive Time!* is on file
  at the Library of Congress.
ISBN 978-1-5415-3906-8 (lib. bdg.)
ISBN 978-1-5415-4659-2 (pbk.)
ISBN 978-1-5415-4358-4 (eb pdf)

Manufactured in the United States of America
1-45089-35916-7/26/2018

TABLE OF CONTENTS

LIFE IN THE FACT LANE

LIGHTNING MCQUEEN AND HIS FOUR-WHEELED FRIENDS ARE ON THE FAST TRACK TO FUN! From race cars to tractors, there's a vehicle for every speed and every need in the world of Cars. And all of them have their own points of view. Sometimes this can lead to terrific teamwork. Other times, it can result in thrilling competition. You never know where the road will lead!

The lists in this book include opinions about some of the best moments from the Cars films. You might agree with some of these opinions. You might disagree with others. No problem! Readers can have their own ideas about the sights to see on this journey. The important thing is that you come along for the ride.

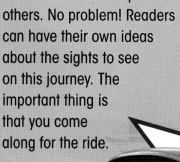

SO BUCKLE UP, AND GET READY TO TAKE A SPIN THROUGH THE WORLD OF CARS. IT'S DRIVE TIME!

TOP 10 THINGS EVERY RACE CAR NEEDS

10 A cool paint job so you stand out from the other racers.

9 The right kind of fuel.

BECAUSE YOU HAVE A NEED FOR SPEED!

8 A corporate sponsor.

THANKS, RUST-EZE AND DINOCO!

7 A worthy opponent.

6 A smart and dedicated trainer.

5 A top-notch, fast-as-lightning pit crew.

^^^^^
DID YOU KNOW?
It takes a lot of people who understand science, technology, engineering, and math to design a race car. It has lots of parts that need to work together and at top speed too!

4

A tough, wise crew chief.

EVEN THE BEST RACER CAN'T DO IT ALONE.

3 A place to race.

A DIRT TRACK, A GRAND PRIX TRACK THROUGH CITY STREETS, A SANDY BEACH, OR EVEN A DRIVING SIMULATOR WILL DO!

2 Focus.

1 CONFIDENCE. "I'M FASTER THAN FAST. QUICKER THAN QUICK. I AM SPEED!" —LIGHTNING MCQUEEN

MATER'S TOP 10 FUNNIEST LINES

10

"Whoa! Git-R-done!"

9

"It goes down faster than elevators full of Winnebagos."

8

"I'm happier than a tornado in a trailer park!"

7

"Hey, I know this might be a bad time right now, but you owe me $32,000 in legal fees."

LEGAL ADVICE IS NOT CHEAP.

8

6

"You are not a nice guy! Though seriously, I gotta say you do make a quality mud flap at an affordable price."

A GOOD MUD FLAP IS HARD TO FIND.

^^^^^
DID YOU KNOW?

The character of Mater is based on a real person who was nicknamed Mater because he loved to eat tomatoes. Mater's design is based on an old, rusty tow truck the filmmakers found when they were doing research for the first *Cars* movie.

5

"I'm startin' to think he knowed you was gonna crash."

MATER THINKS DOC HUDSON IS PRETTY SMART.

4

"You know what I'd do? . . . I don't know. I got nothin'."

3

"Whatever you do, *do not* eat the free pistachio ice cream."

2

"I'm a precisional instrument of speed and aromatics."

JUST ONE OF THE MANY REASONS TO LOVE MATER.

1

"MY NAME'S MATER . . . LIKE *TUH-MATER*, BUT WITHOUT THE *TUH*."

LIGHTNING'S TOP 10 FRIENDSHIP MOMENTS

10 Lightning and Cruz race on the beach together.

THEY REALLY DO MAKE A GREAT TEAM.

9 Lightning and a rocket-propelled Mater race together in the Radiator Springs Grand Prix.

8 Lightning still thinks of Doc, even after he's gone.

DOC WAS THE BEST MENTOR AND CREW CHIEF AROUND!

7

Sally and Lightning go for a drive.

AND SHE SHOWS HIM THAT SPECTACULAR VIEW!

6 Mater becomes Lightning's biggest cheerleader.

MATER HAS ALL THE FAN LOOT: A FOAM LIGHTNING BOLT, A BIG WIG, AND A RACETRACK HAT.

∧∧∧∧∧

DID YOU KNOW?

Rust is no friend to a car or truck. Over time, water can cause metal to form a flaky coating called rust. The rust slowly eats away at the metal. Rusted metal can become so weak and thin that it falls apart easily.

5 Mater takes Lightning out tractor tipping.

4 Lightning tells Mater to be himself no matter where they are.

BEST FRIENDS LIKE YOU JUST THE WAY YOU ARE.

3 When all of his Radiator Springs friends show up to be Lightning's pit crew against Chick and the King.

2 Lightning helps Mater get a ride in the Dinoco helicopter.

DAD-GUM, THAT'S FUN!

1 **MATER CALLS LIGHTNING HIS BEST FRIEND FOR THE FIRST TIME. "I KNOWED I MADE A GOOD CHOICE . . . [IN] MY BEST FRIEND."**

TOP 10 THINGS TO SEE AND DO IN RADIATOR SPRINGS

10 Have your picture taken next to the Leaning Tower of Tires at Luigi's Casa Della Tires.

9 Change your colors at Ramone's House of Body Art.

8 See a movie at the Radiator Springs Drive-In Theatre.

WHO WOULDN'T WANT TO SEE *TOY CAR STORY* OR *MONSTER TRUCKS, INC.*?

7 Check out the Radiator Springs Racing Museum.

6 Go tractor tipping in the pasture.
WATCH OUT FOR FRANK!

5 Take a drive through Ornament Valley. Or check out the mountains of the Cadillac Range.

4 Stay at the Cozy Cone Motel.
SALLY HAS A ROOM WAITING FOR YOU.

2 Have a snack at Flo's V8 Cafe.
FLO WILL TAKE GOOD CARE OF YOU!

∧∧∧∧∧
DID YOU KNOW?
The town of Radiator Springs was founded by a steam car named Stanley. He married a Model T car named Lizzie, who still runs the town's souvenir shop. The Stanley Steamer was actually a steam-powered car used in races in the early twentieth century, and Tin Lizzie was the nickname for inventor Henry Ford's Model T car.

3 Buy a bumper sticker from Lizzie at her Radiator Springs Curios shop.

1

CRUISE DOWN THE MAIN STREET AND ENJOY THE NEON LIGHTS.

TOP 10 WAYS TO GET LIGHTNING MCQUEEN TO LOSE HIS COOL

10 Stop timing him on the beach to protect a little crab in the sand. **OH, BUT CRABS ARE SO CUTE!**

9

Accidentally win a demolition derby when you're supposed to be helping him train for a race. **JUST STAY AWAY FROM MISS FRITTER!**

8 Tell him he's too old to keep racing.

7

Beat him in a race.

HE HATES THAT. JUST ASK JACKSON STORM.

6 Make him pull a paving machine to put asphalt on a road.

5 Make him scrape asphalt off a road when he puts it on wrong.

4 Tell him to turn right to go left without explaining what that means.

THANKS, DOC. VERY HELPFUL.

3 Insult his racing skills.

2 Keep him from getting to the racetrack on time.

1 FORCE HIM TO RETIRE BEFORE HE'S READY.

HE DECIDES WHEN HE'S DONE RACING.

TOP 10 HIGH-OCTANE RACES

10

The race through London. Good thing Holley Shiftwell installed those rocket boosters on Mater!

9 The race through Italy. **KEEP AN EYE OUT FOR LEMONS!**

8 The race through Japan. Mater with a headset turns out not to be such a great idea.

7 The race when a young Doc Hudson has a terrible crash.

6 The tiebreaking "Race of the Century" with Lightning McQueen, Chick Hicks, and the King.

"BOOGITY, BOOGITY, BOOGITY!" —DARRELL CARTRIP

5 The Crazy 8 race at Thunder Hollow.

4 When Lightning McQueen races Jackson Storm on the simulator—and crashes through the screen.

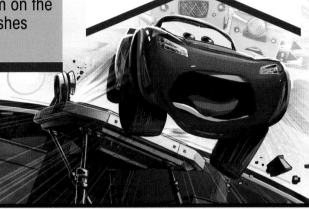

3 The Florida 500 race at the Florida International Super Speedway.

CRUZ FINALLY REALIZES HER DREAM.

2 The Piston Cup three-way tie between Lightning McQueen, Chick Hicks, and the King.

1

DOC AND LIGHTNING MCQUEEN'S EPIC RACE AROUND WILLY'S BUTTE.

QUIZ BREAK!

Can you cross the finish line with winning answers for this Cars quiz?

1

WHAT IS THE NAME OF LIGHTNING MCQUEEN'S TRANSPORT TRUCK?

A Minny
B Mack
C Mater
D Macaroni

2

WHAT COLOR WAS MATER BEFORE HE TURNED RUSTY?

A Red
B Yellow
C Light blue
D Purple

3

WHO WINS THE PISTON CUP BY HITTING ANOTHER RACER?

A Lightning McQueen
B The King
C Doc Hudson
D Chick Hicks

LIGHTNING MCQUEEN'S FAMOUS CATCHPHRASE IS

A Ka-chow!
B Woo-hoo!
C Boo-yah!
D Yee-haw!

4

5

WHICH OF THESE IS NOT THE NAME OF A CARS CHARACTER?

A Chick Hicks
B Ivan
C Smokey
D Andy

6

IN *CARS*, WHAT DOES MATER TAKE A RIDE IN?

A A helicopter
B A train
C A Winnebago
D A transport truck

7

WHAT KIND OF CAR IS DOC HUDSON?

A Hudson Hawk
B Blue Bomber
C Hudson Hornet
D Road Rally Racer

8

WHO RUNS THE COZY CONE MOTEL?

A Flo
B Sally Carrera
C Lizzie
D Luigi

9

WHAT IS CRUZ RAMIREZ'S DREAM JOB?

A Trainer for the best young racers
B Pit crew chief
C Attorney
D Racer

TOP 10 QUOTES FROM CARS FRIENDS

10

"You can use anything negative as fuel to push through to the positive."
—Cruz

9

"You got a lotta stuff, kid." —Doc

8

"You are a racer. Use that."

LIGHTNING GIVES CRUZ THE CONFIDENCE SHE NEEDS IN HER FIRST RACE.

7

"Hud saw something in you that you didn't even see in yourself."
—Smokey

The animators at Pixar used a special technique called ray tracing to show reflections of other objects on the metallic bodies of the cars.

6

"I've wanted to become a racer forever. Because of you." —Cruz

5

"Lightning wins. He decides when he's done racing. That was the deal. Hi, I'm his lawyer."

SALLY TAKING CARE OF BUSINESS.

4

"The racing *is* the reward. Not the stuff!" —Lightning

3

"Life's too short to take no for an answer." —Louise

2

"Racing wasn't the best part of Hud's life. You were."

SMOKEY TELLING LIGHTNING HOW DOC REALLY FELT.

1

"DON'T FEAR FAILURE. BE AFRAID OF NOT HAVING THE CHANCE. YOU HAVE THE CHANCE." —SALLY

TOP 10 QUOTES FROM TROUBLEMAKERS AND BAD GUYS

10 "MOOOOO!"

UH-OH! HERE COMES FRANK!

9 "We got ourselves a *nodder*." —Boost

8 "Hey, McQueen, that must be really embarrassing. But I wouldn't worry about it . . . because I didn't do it! Ha Ha Ha!" —Chick Hicks

7 "I'm about to commit a movin' violation!" —Miss Fritter

6 "You have no idea what a pleasure it is for me to finally beat you."

YES, JACKSON STORM SAID BEAT.

5 "The next time he makes a stop, instead of saying 'ka-chow,' he's gonna go 'ka-boom!'"

ACER THINKS HE'S SO CLEVER.

∧∧∧∧∧
DID YOU KNOW?

Chick Hicks is covered with more than three hundred stickers. Real race cars are covered with stickers and decals too. In fact, many race cars are covered with huge decal wraps instead of paint. This makes the cars lighter and faster.

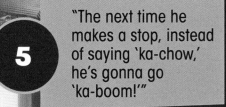

4 "No! You DON'T belong on this track!" Jackson Storm wants Cruz out of the way—and out of the race.

3 "You actually care about that race car. A pity you didn't warn him in time." —Professor Zündapp

2 "You're insane, you are! Deactivate!"

MILES AXLEROD HAS TO STOP HIS OWN EVIL PLAN.

1

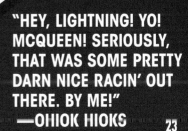

"HEY, LIGHTNING! YO! MCQUEEN! SERIOUSLY, THAT WAS SOME PRETTY DARN NICE RACIN' OUT THERE. BY ME!"
—CHICK HICKS

TOP 10 EDGE-OF-YOUR-SEAT SCENES

10 Mater and Lightning McQueen get chased by Frank after tractor tipping.

9 Lightning McQueen flips out of control in the last race of the season.

8 Mater escapes from the secret lemon summit meeting.

THAT WAS A CLOSE CALL!

7

Smokey and the Legends take Lightning and Cruz into the woods to race in the dark.

6 Chick Hicks causes the King to crash.

THAT'S NO WAY TO WIN.

5 Mater, Finn McMissile, and Holley Shiftwell get trapped inside Big Bentley.

DAD-GUM! DAD-GUM! DAD-GUM!

4 Cruz and Lightning McQueen try to survive the Crazy 8 race.

3 When the bomb attached to Mater ticks down to its final seconds.

2 When Cruz flips over Jackson Storm to win the race.

SHE REALLY IS A RACER!

1 LIGHTNING MCQUEEN RACES JACKSON STORM, LOSES CONTROL, AND CRASHES. OUCH! THAT HAD TO HURT—IN MORE WAYS THAN ONE.

TOP 10 CARS FUN FACTS

10 The characters' license plates have hidden meanings.

FOR EXAMPLE, DOC IS A 1951 HUDSON HORNET AND A MEDICAL DOCTOR, SO HIS PLATES SAY 51HHMD.

9 Animators made more than forty-three thousand sketches of cars for the first *Cars* movie.

8 The jet tails in the movies' sky scenes are actually tire tracks!

7 Flo's V8 Cafe looks like the V-shaped parts of a car engine.

ONE ORDER OF OIL, COMING RIGHT UP!

6

The rocky hills around Radiator Springs are shaped like old car parts.

5

Lightning McQueen's 95 stands for 1995, the year *Toy Story* was made.

LIGHTNING AND MATER, WOODY AND BUZZ—FANTASTIC FRIENDS, AWESOME ADVENTURES!

4

Life-size, remote-control versions of Lightning McQueen, Mater, Finn McMissile, Cruz Ramirez, and Jackson Storm were used to advertise the Cars movies.

3

Mater is the only Cars character with crooked teeth.

2

The Piston Cup trophy is shaped like an engine piston with wings attached.

PISTONS HELP A CAR'S ENGINE GO, GO, GO!

1

THE IDEA FOR *CARS* CAME FROM AN OLD CARTOON ABOUT A LITTLE BLUE CAR.

TOP 10 WINNING TIPS FROM DOC HUDSON

10

"You look! All I see is a bunch of empty cups."

YOU RACE BECAUSE YOU LOVE IT, NOT FOR TROPHIES!

9

"You give it too much throttle, and you're in the tulips."

STAY OUTTA THOSE TULIPS.

8

"Ha, that ain't racing. That wasn't even a Sunday drive. That was one lap. Racing is five hundred of those."

7

"Find a groove that works for you and get that lap back."

6

"If I were you, I'd quit yappin' and start workin'."

ALWAYS GOOD ADVICE!

^^^^^^
DID YOU KNOW?

The 1951 Hudson Hornet was a famous race car. It had the biggest, most powerful engine of any American car of its time. Its power and design helped it win almost every race it entered.

5

"I knew you needed a crew chief, but I didn't know it was this bad."

EVERYBODY NEEDS A LITTLE HELP SOMETIMES.

4

"All right, if you can drive as good as you can fix a road, then you can win this race with your eyes shut. Now get back out there."

YOU CAN'T WIN A RACE IF YOU'RE NOT ON THE RACETRACK!

3

"When is the last time you cared about something except yourself, hot rod?"

2

"I didn't come all this way to see you quit."

1

"IF YOU'RE GOIN' HARD ENOUGH LEFT, YOU'LL FIND YOURSELF TURNIN' RIGHT."

LEARN HOW TO DO WHAT YOU NEED TO DO TO GET WHERE YOU WANT TO BE.

MAKE YOUR OWN CARS TOP 10!

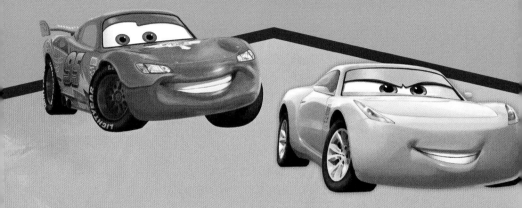

IT'S YOUR TURN TO BE IN THE TOP 10 DRIVER'S SEAT!
Make a copy of the blank list on the next page. Then make your own Cars Top 10 list. Rewrite one of the lists from this book. Or make a whole new list instead, such as

- **THE TOP 10 BEST THINGS ABOUT BEING A CAR**

- **THE TOP 10 LIGHTNING AND CRUZ MOMENTS**

Take your creativity out for a spin, and cruise through your own winning Top 10 lists!

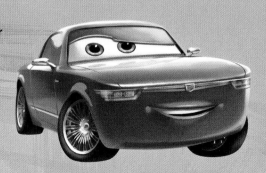

COPY THIS PAGE!

MY

Disney · PIXAR

Cars

TOP 10:

10. _____

9. _____

8. _____

7. _____

6. _____

5. _____

4. _____

3. _____

2. _____

1. _____

TO LEARN MORE

Books

Heiman, Larry. *The Science of Cars: A Cars Discovery Book.*
Minneapolis: Lerner Publications, 2019.
Read this book to learn more about your favorite Cars characters
and the science behind how they work!

Meet the Cars. Los Angeles: Disney Press, 2017.
Get to know a whole crew of vehicles from the Cars world in this
book, including characters from all three films.

Websites

Disney Pixar Cars
https://cars.disney.com
Make a pit stop at this website to find Cars videos, games,
activities, picture galleries, and more!

Pixar: *Cars 3*
https://www.pixar.com/feature-films/cars-3/#cars-3-main-2
Find out about the characters, creative thinking, and clever design
decisions that went into the making of *Cars 3.*